Applying the Kingdom
40-Day
Devotional Journal

OTHER BOOKS
BY MYLES MUNROE

AVAILABLE FROM DESTINY IMAGE PUBLISHERS

Applying the Kingdom 40-Day Devotional Journal

Myles Munroe

Compiled by Jan Sherman.

Destiny Image® Publishers, Inc.
P.O. Box 310
Shippensburg, PA 17257-0310

"Speaking to the Purposes of God for this Generation and for the Generations to Come."

Bahamas Faith Ministry
P.O. Box N9583
Nassau, Bahamas

For Worldwide Distribution, Printed in the U.S.A.

ISBN 10: 0-7684-2671-5
ISBN 13: 978-0-7684-2671-7

This book and all other Destiny Image, Revival Press, MercyPlace, Fresh Bread, Destiny Image Fiction, and Treasure House books are available at Christian bookstores and distributors worldwide.

For a U.S. bookstore nearest you, call **1-800-722-6774.**
For more information on foreign distributors, call **717-532-3040.**
Reach us on the Internet: **www.destinyimage.com.**

1 2 3 4 5 6 7 8 9 10 / 12 11 10 09 08

Contents

The Keys to Life

THEREFORE I TELL YOU, DO NOT WORRY ABOUT YOUR LIFE, WHAT YOU WILL EAT OR DRINK; OR ABOUT YOUR BODY, WHAT YOU WILL WEAR. IS NOT LIFE MORE IMPORTANT THAN FOOD, AND THE BODY MORE IMPORTANT THAN CLOTHES? (MATTHEW 6:25).

TODAY'S DEVOTION

Every human is searching for the simple formula to a successful, fulfilled life. He or she wants to find the one key that unlocks the door to the good life and answers the questions of their heart.

So what is the key to life? Finding your true purpose and living it. Let me sum this up in four statements that all relate to purpose—four "keys" to understanding the difference between a purpose-filled life and a life with no meaning.

One: The greatest tragedy in life is not death, but life without a purpose. Finding our purpose in life is critically important.

Two: The greatest challenge in life is knowing what to do. We go about our daily activities, but are we doing what we are supposed to be doing?

Three: The greatest mistake in life is being busy, but not effective. Being busy is a common human pastime, but that doesn't mean that what you're doing is worth doing. We must learn how to live effectively without being busy.

Four: The greatest failure in life is being successful in the wrong assignment. Success alone is not enough. You must succeed in the right thing. Succeeding in the wrong assignment is failure.

(Excerpt: *Applying the Kingdom*, Chapter 1)

QUESTIONS

1. Are you doing what you are supposed to be doing? Do you even know what to do? These are tough questions, but learning the answers is vital to your future.

2. Why is the greatest tragedy in life not death, but life without a purpose? How does this affect everything that we do?

3. Why is the greatest challenge in life knowing what to do? Do you know what to do with your life? What drive gets you out of bed every morning? What purpose propels you through each day? Are you living for a paycheck? Or are you living for a purpose?

4. Why is the greatest mistake in life being busy, but not effective? What is the measure of effectiveness in your life? Do you feel you are effective in most of what you do?

5. Why is the greatest failure in life being successful in the wrong assignment? Do you know your assignment? Do you know what you have accomplished thus far toward the fulfillment of your assignment?

MEDITATION

"If a teacher gives you a test and instructs you to answer only the odd-numbered questions, and you answer the even-numbered questions instead, even if you answer every question correctly, you will still fail because you didn't follow instructions. You succeeded in the wrong assignment, which means you failed. God is not impressed with our sincerity, faithfulness, commitment, or success unless we are pursuing the right assignment—His assignment. Anything else is failure."

Have you been guilty of trying to impress God with your sincerity, faithfulness, commitment, or success, but on the wrong assignment? Why do you think we presume we can fool God in this way?

Establishing Priorities: The Key to Success

So do not worry, saying, "What shall we eat?" or "What shall we drink?" or "What shall we wear?" For the pagans run after all these things, and your heavenly Father knows that you need them (Matthew 6:31,32).

TODAY'S DEVOTION

Success in life is the effective use of time. Learning to establish priorities is a critical key to effective time management. Priorities help us to avoid distractions, focus on the most important things, and to get the most value out of our time every day. Each of us is the sum total of what we spend our time on.

Time is the currency of life. How we spend our time determines the quality of our life and death. In a very real sense we become what we spend our time on.

Because time is currency and a precious commodity, it should come as no surprise to discover that everything and everyone is after our time. Some of it is worthwhile and deserves our attention; most of it does not.

How do we tell the difference? Without clear priorities, we run the danger of wasting precious time listening to the wrong voices or allowing ourselves to be drawn in the wrong direction.

The key to success is effective use of time, and the key to effective use of time is knowing the correct priorities. The only way to spend your time currency effectively is to identify the correct priorities for your life.

(Excerpt: *Applying the Kingdom,* Chapter 1)

QUESTIONS

1. How effective do you think you are at using your time? At the end of the day, do you feel that circumstances and people controlled you more than your goals and agenda?

2. If the measure of who we are is how we have used our time, how do you feel about your life in general? How will people feel when you die? Will they be sad...or relieved?

3. *How does the currency of time affect the decisions you make on a daily basis? Do you tend to misspend the currency afforded to you in the 24 hours of each day? Do you find it to be true that time is money?*

4. How have you made priorities in your life? How did you determine the importance of these activities or goals? Was this an easy or difficult process?

5. What are your current priorities for your life? How well do you spend your time on these items?

MEDITATION

"God is not impressed with busyness. The only way to live effectively is to use your time on the correct priorities for your life. Some of your priorities may be good, but not correct. It is important to learn the difference. Time wasted on incorrect priorities is currency that is gone forever. It can never be regained."

Do you have the correct priorities for your life? Take time to go before the Lord to allow Him to confirm the priorities you have, and to make changes in the ones that need His alterations, and provide new priorities according to His will and purpose.

The Priority of Priority

B UT SEEK FIRST HIS KINGDOM AND HIS RIGH-
TEOUSNESS, AND ALL THESE THINGS WILL BE
GIVEN TO YOU AS WELL (MATTHEW 6:33).

TODAY'S DEVOTION

There are numerous significant reasons for establishing priorities:

• *Preoccupation with priority preserves and protects life.* Doing the right thing at the right time in the right way keeps us from doing the wrong thing at the wrong time in the wrong way.

- *Correct priority is the principle of progress.* True progress is measured not by how much we get done but by whether or not we are moving in the right direction.

- *Correct priority protects time.*

- *Correct priority protects energy.* We should strive not to be busy, but to be correct.

- *Correct priority protects talents and gifts.* Priorities will help you avoid expending your talents and gifts on unworthy endeavors.

- *Correct priority protects decisions.* Setting your heart on God's priority will enable you to choose the right course and maximize your life's effectiveness.

- *Correct priority protects discipline.* Priority-induced discipline protects you from wasting your time, energy, effort, talents, gifts and, especially, your life.

- *Correct priority simplifies life.*

We tend to prioritize our lives around things: food, drink, clothing, a paycheck, a car, a house. But the Kingdom of Heaven was the singular focus of Jesus' life and message.

And it must be our priority as well. First things first!

(Excerpt: *Applying the Kingdom,* Chapter 1)

QUESTIONS

1. There are eight significant reasons for establishing priorities listed above. Using the chart below, note information that will help you in your life's pursuit.

Reason for Establishing Priorities	What This Means to Me	Things I Might Be Able to Benefit From
preserves and protects life		

MEDITATION

"What was the secret to Jesus' amazingly effective life?
He reduced all of life to two simple pursuits:
(1) a Kingdom from a place called Heaven, and
(2) a concept He called 'righteousness.' In fact,
for the entire duration of His earthly ministry,
He focused only on these two subjects and related all
of His principles, precepts, laws, and instructions to them."

If you were to reduce your life to two pursuits, what would they be? How well do your time management and prioritization process reflect these two pursuits? Ask God to help you improve in your effectiveness.

The Danger of Misplaced Priority

WHERE THERE IS NO REVELATION [VISION], THE PEOPLE CAST OFF RESTRAINT (PROVERBS 29:18A).

TODAY'S DEVOTION

Singularity of purpose and clarity of priorities caused Jesus to stand out so clearly among the people of His day. Unlike Jesus, people in general have a problem putting first things first.

Absence of priority causes one to drift through life with no focus or sense of purpose or direction. All of one's energy and potential are dissipated by trying to shoot off in too many directions and trying to do too many things. In many cases, people with no priority become lethargic and apathetic. A dull sameness characterizes their day-to-day living.

Here are some results of the absence of priority:

- the wasting of time and energy.
- becoming busy on the wrong things.
- spending time doing the unnecessary.
- majoring on the unimportant.
- preoccupation with the unimportant.
- investing in the less valuable.
- ineffective activity.
- the abuse of gifts and talents.
- forfeiting purpose.
- failure.

Nothing is more tragic than a life without purpose. If purpose is not known, priorities cannot be established and nothing worthwhile in life can be accomplished. No matter what we think about life, we have to live it every day and give an account of our management.

(Excerpt: *Applying the Kingdom*, Chapter 2)

QUESTIONS

1. What are some of the ways in which Jesus showed His singular purpose? What was that purpose? What does Jesus' life model for your life?

2. When a disciple, opportunity, or other factor attempted to distract Jesus from His focus, what was His response? What is your response to distractions?

3. Have you ever felt that your life seemed to be adrift, without purpose? Or do you know someone who has had this feeling? What are ways that we can address these feelings to align with God's purpose for us?

4. Look at the list of results when there is an absence of priority on one's life. Are there any that are descriptive of your life, past or present? How can following priorities eliminate these issues?

5. Why is purpose so important in establishing priorities? What is your purpose? What can you do to eliminate things that distract you from your purpose and your priorities?

MEDITATION

"No matter how successful you are in what you do,
if you are not doing the most important thing—the
thing that you are supposed to be doing—you are
failing. Busy activity, sweat, and hard work are important,
as long as you are focused on the right assignment. However,
they can never substitute for correct priority. Priorities are
like river banks, in that they control the flow of life."

Take some time to ask the Lord to direct your priorities. Think through the implications of each assignment you have currently, and ask Him to direct your path.

Misplaced Priority: Meeting Personal Needs

And why do you worry about clothes? See how the lilies of the field grow. They do not labor or spin. Yet I tell you that not even Solomon in all his splendor was dressed like one of these. If that is how God clothes the grass of the field, which is here today and tomorrow is thrown into the fire, will He not much more clothe you, O you of little faith? (Matthew 6:28-30)

TODAY'S DEVOTION

From the creation of the human race, the Creator established the priority of man when He commanded man to focus on dominion over the earth. That changed when man lost dominion through disobedience. Evicted from the Garden, Adam and Eve had to pay attention to things they had once taken for granted, such as food, water, shelter, and even survival itself.

This tragic event initiated the change in priorities for all mankind and refocused his life on daily survival. This preoccupation with temporal, fundamental needs has consumed people to this day.

Everything man does outside the Kingdom of Heaven is motivated by the drive to meet personal needs.

Man separated in spirit from God and invented religion as a vehicle to find the lost kingdom state of rulership and control the earth's resources to meet his needs.

Religion is selfish because all religion is driven by the priority of needs. The promise of meeting needs is the main reason people stay in a religion. Even when a religion fails to deliver what it promises, its followers are reluctant to leave it because faith in tradition dies hard.

Mankind in general suffers from the dual dilemma of misplaced priority and misplaced faith.

(Excerpt: *Applying the Kingdom,* Chapter 2)

DAY 5—*Misplaced Priority: Meeting Personal Needs*

QUESTIONS

1. What do you think life would be like if meeting basic needs was not the focus? How would we prioritize our days? What other things would change?

2. When man exchanged dominion over the earth for being dominated by earthly needs, what did that say about man's rebellion? When we make the same exchange today, what are we telling God?

3. *If "everything outside the Kingdom of Heaven is motivated by the drive to meet basic needs," how much is the Christian's life affected by outside motivations? How are we to live?*

4. What role does religion play in the lives of people? Why do they think religion will meet their needs? Why doesn't it meet their expectations?

5. How is religion selfish? How can Christianity become religious in nature just like other religions? How can we avoid this?

MEDITATION

"In all religions, religious priority in petition and prayer is for personal needs. Let's be honest. For most of us, 99 percent of our prayers deal with what we want from God: a new job, new car, new house, enough money not only to pay the bills but also to gratify our lust for things. How often do we spare a thought for what He wants?"

Reflect as to how much of your prayers are taken up with requests to meet our needs or wants. How often do you ask what God wants? Make time to ask God in your prayer time today.

Paganism Is Alive and Well

YOU WILL KEEP HIM IN PERFECT PEACE, WHOSE MIND IS STAYED [STEADFAST] ON YOU, BECAUSE HE TRUSTS IN YOU (ISAIAH 26:3 NKJV).

TODAY'S DEVOTION

Most people approach life in one of two ways: either they work to live or they live to work. Jesus said that both approaches are wrong.

Any religion that focuses on the acquisition of things and the meeting of personal needs is a religion of pagans. Based on that definition, paganism is alive and well in our world today. One of the largest gatherings of pagans takes places every Sunday when the communities known as the church of Jesus Christ gather for worship.

We claim to trust God, but our daily lives reveal that most do not. Our preoccupation with material things, satisfying basic needs and getting ahead is nothing other than pagan behavior.

This does not mean that we should quit our jobs and sit around waiting for God to drop all of these things in our laps. It does mean that as we work day to day we are living for God's priorities, confident that He has us covered. There is no surer antidote to stress and worry.

It is time to set aside the pagan mind-set with its priority of things and take up instead the divine priority, the priority of the Kingdom of God.

(Excerpt: *Applying the Kingdom,* Chapter 2)

QUESTIONS

1. Do you think you work to live or do you live to work? Think about some of your closest friends or relationships? Do they fall under either of these? Why are both wrong?

2. Why do you think that a pagan religion focuses on the acquisition of things and the meeting of personal needs? Why are these things so defining as to how pagan religions work?

3. Do you agree with the author that paganism exists on Sunday mornings in many of our churches? Why or why not? How does the author make such a claim?

4. How is preoccupation with material things a matter of trust? When we are preoccupied who are we trusting? Who are we *not* trusting?

5. Have you known people who believe that to trust God means that they should sit and wait for God to give them what they need? Why is this type of thinking wrong? What should our stance be in terms of working and trusting God?

MEDITATION

"Our problem is that we have misplaced our faith. We have changed our source. Instead of looking to our heavenly Father, we look either to ourselves or to someone else to sustain us. If you are looking to anyone other than God the Father as your source, that may explain why you are struggling. If you make God your source, then He calls the shots. And if He calls the shots, He pays the bills!"

Who is your source? Have you misplaced your faith in a source other than God? If you have done so, even in a small area of your life, make your confession and seek His forgiveness.

The Priority of God—"Kingdom First!"

BUT SEEK HIS KINGDOM, AND THESE THINGS WILL BE GIVEN TO YOU AS WELL (LUKE 12:31).

TODAY'S DEVOTION

Our greatest longing is also God's primary intent and desire. God's highest priority is restoring the Kingdom of Heaven on earth. It was to this end that He sent His Son, Jesus Christ, to become one of us. Jesus' message was simple and straightforward: "Repent, for the kingdom of heaven is near" (Matt. 4:17b). He instructed His followers to "seek first His [God's] kingdom and His righteousness, and all these things will be given to you as well" (Matt. 6:33).

The Kingdom of Heaven was the central theme of everything Jesus did and said. And that message of the Kingdom is the same message the world needs to hear today because everyone on earth is searching for the Kingdom of Heaven.

The "Kingdom first!" message so universal and so important because when we understand "Kingdom first!" we will understand how to live effectively. Everybody wants to live effectively. We all want our lives to mean something. Each of us desires to control our own destiny, live out our dreams, and fulfill our highest potential. Understanding and embracing the "Kingdom first!" message will make these things possible. It will allow us to understand the keys to life.

(Excerpt: *Applying the Kingdom,* Chapter 2)

QUESTIONS

1. How do you know that God's highest priority is restoring the Kingdom of Heaven on earth? What cues do you have from what Jesus said and did?

2. Do you agree with the author that the world is searching for the Kingdom of God? Why or why not? How do people search for the Kingdom of God? In what ways do they substitute other things for the Kingdom? Why don't these things satisfy?

3. What does the "Kingdom first!" message mean to you? How would you explain it to someone else? What does a "Kingdom first!" person think about?

4. When someone has a "Kingdom first!" lifestyle, how do they show it? Would this lifestyle be intriguing to someone who is not in the Kingdom? Why or why not?

5. How does embracing the "Kingdom first!" message allow us to understand the keys to life? Has this been true in your own life?

35

MEDITATION

"'Kingdom first!' is a message with universal application. It relates to everyone on earth. 'Kingdom first!' is a message for Christians, Jews, Muslims, Buddhists and Hindus. It is for atheists and agnostics. It is for scientists, theologians, and philosophers. 'Kingdom first!' is a message for people of every religion and people of no religion because it is not a religious message. 'Kingdom first!' is a message that transcends religion."

How can the "Kingdom first!" message transcend all religions? How can the message break through to those who are in pagan religions? How might you practice the "Kingdom first!" message so you can relay it to others?

The Exclusiveness of the Divine Priority

No one can serve two masters. Either he will hate the one and love the other, or he will be devoted to the one and despise the other. You cannot serve both God and money (Matthew 6:24).

TODAY'S DEVOTION

Jesus says that when we make the Kingdom of God our one priority, all the other things that we have spent our lives pursuing will turn around and pursue us! They will chase us down! This is a fundamental principle of the Kingdom of God.

Kingdom-possessed people do not live just to make a living; they live for the Kingdom. Kingdom-possessed people do not work just to get a paycheck; they work for the Kingdom. Kingdom-possessed people do not strive day in and day out to meet their needs; they strive continually for the Kingdom. For Kingdom-possessed people, all of life is about the Kingdom of God.

The Kingdom of God is so vast that our pursuit of it will fill us to capacity so that we have no room for other priorities. It also will satisfy us so completely that we have no need of other priorities. All the priorities that we recognize as essential or beneficial to life will be satisfied when we set our hearts to seek first the Kingdom of God. This is His promise to us. But He requires our exclusive allegiance. He demands from us our whole heart, our undivided loyalty.

(Excerpt: *Applying the Kingdom,* Chapter 3)

QUESTIONS

1. What does the author mean when he says, "When we make the Kingdom of God our one priority, all the other things that we have spent our lives pursuing will turn around and pursue us"? Have you found yourself "chased down" by the items that most people pursue?

2. Reflect on the way Kingdom possessed people lead a different type of life than those outside the Kingdom. Fill in the chart with information given above to help you.

	Does not	Does
A Kingdom possessed person		
A Kingdom possessed person		
A Kingdom possessed person		

3. Why do you think Kingdom possessed people operate under the principle that "all of life is about the Kingdom of God"? Do you feel you operate under this principle?

4. How does the Kingdom of God squeeze out other priorities in the lives of those who are possessed by it? What priorities did the Kingdom of God squeeze out of your life?

5. How does the Kingdom of God satisfy those who are possessed by it so that other priorities are not needed? What needs were replaced by the satisfaction of the Kingdom of God in your life?

MEDITATION

"By our Manufacturer's design, we are not equipped to serve two masters. One will always take precedence over the other. There is room in our hearts for one and only one top priority, and Jesus said that top priority must be the Kingdom of God. This is why He said we are to seek first God's Kingdom and righteousness."

Why are we incapable of serving two masters? Do you find a struggle within yourself as to whom or what you serve because of the press of life? Renew your commitment to allow Jesus to be Lord over your life and make the Kingdom of God your first priority.

The Peril of Divided Loyalty

A S THEY WERE WALKING ALONG THE ROAD, A MAN SAID TO HIM, "I WILL FOLLOW YOU WHEREVER YOU GO." JESUS REPLIED, "FOXES HAVE HOLES AND BIRDS OF THE AIR HAVE NESTS, BUT THE SON OF MAN HAS NO PLACE TO LAY HIS HEAD" (LUKE 9:57-58).

TODAY'S DEVOTION

The Kingdom priority is exclusive with regard to the cost it exacts from us. Although seeking first the Kingdom of God results in the most fulfilling and rewarding life possible, that does not mean it is always easy. What does the King demand from us? Everything. But the rewards are well worth the cost.

We cannot call Christ "Lord," and then say, "But first let me do such and such." If He is Lord, there is no "first"; there is only "yes." Either He owns us or He does not. Either He is our Master or He is not. The Kingdom priority does not allow for divided loyalty. It makes an exclusive claim on our lives.

The Kingdom priority claims our all. There is no room in the Kingdom of God for a spirit of ownership.

A spirit of ownership is perhaps the greatest external sign that someone is not in the Kingdom or not yet walking in the priority of "Kingdom first!" If God cannot ask for and take from us anything He wants anytime He wants without us putting up a fight, then He is not our Lord, no matter what we claim.

(Excerpt: *Applying the Kingdom*, Chapter 3)

QUESTIONS

1. Did you understand the cost of coming into the Kingdom of God when you decided to do so? What was your understanding of the price of being in the Kingdom?

2. When you first came into the Kingdom of God, what rewards did you expect to receive? Did you receive these rewards?

3. What does God demand from His Kingdom citizens? How does this make life not easy? How does it make life rewarding?

4. How does making Jesus our Lord make Him first in our lives? How does His Lordship demand only "yes" answers? How does His Lordship require immediate response from us?

5. In your opinion, what is the spirit of ownership? How does this spirit stand, opposed to the Kingdom of God? Have you had trouble with this spirit at any time in your life?

MEDITATION

"The Kingdom priority is exclusive with regard to our relationships, particularly with family. Honoring one's parents is so important that God established it as the fifth commandment.

"God's promise to provide 'all these things' when we seek first His Kingdom includes caring for the family we may have to leave behind in order to follow God's call. If we take care of the Kingdom, the King will take care of our family."

Have you ever had to forego family for the sake of the Kingdom of God? When we make such a choice, what does it take to remain true to the priority of the Kingdom?

Nothing We Give Up for the Kingdom Is Ever Lost

PETER SAID TO HIM, "WE HAVE LEFT ALL WE HAD TO FOLLOW YOU!" "I TELL YOU THE TRUTH," JESUS SAID TO THEM, "NO ONE WHO HAS LEFT HOME OR WIFE OR BROTHERS OR PARENTS OR CHILDREN FOR THE SAKE OF THE KINGDOM OF GOD WILL FAIL TO RECEIVE MANY TIMES AS MUCH IN THIS AGE AND, IN THE AGE TO COME, ETERNAL LIFE" (LUKE 18:28–30).

TODAY'S DEVOTION

After the bombshell Jesus dropped about the difficulty of rich people entering the Kingdom of God, Peter may have been feeling a little uncertain about his own status. So he reminded Jesus that he and the rest of Jesus' disciples had left everything in order to follow Him. This may have been Peter's not-so-subtle way of asking, "What's in it for us?"

Jesus' answer reveals that the exclusive nature of the Kingdom priority is not as risky or as outrageous as it may seem at first. In essence, whatever we give to the King for the sake of His Kingdom, He will multiply and return to us. The more we give, the more we will receive, not for our own lusts or greedy desires, but so we can seek His Kingdom even more and help others to do so as well.

Jesus said, "Seek first His kingdom and His righteousness, and all these things will be given to you as well" (Matt.6:33). The Kingdom priority is exclusive, but it is not limited. God wants you to have "all these things"; He just doesn't want them to have you. So forsake everything for the sake of God's Kingdom. Give Him your all, and He will give you "all these things."

(Excerpt: *Applying the Kingdom,* Chapter 3)

QUESTIONS

1. Look at Luke 9:28-30 above. Have you ever felt like you needed to remind the Lord about what you have given up for the Kingdom of God?

2. What is the exclusive nature of the Kingdom of God? Does the exclusivity mean that it is difficult to get in? Is it difficult to keep your status in the Kingdom of God? What does it mean?

3. What does the author mean when he says, "Whatever we give to the King for the sake of His Kingdom, He will multiply and return to us. The more we give, the more we will receive, not for our own lusts or greedy desires, but so we can seek His Kingdom even more, and help others to do so as well"? Is this true in your experience?

4. How is the Kingdom of God not limited by anything? How should this truth affect the way we perceive our situations on earth and respond to them?

5. How can we trust God to keep us from having those things that could "have us"? What are ways to pray so that we don't get anything that might "trip us up"?

MEDITATION

*"One reason we should be able to give up the
spirit of ownership is because nothing we give up
for the Kingdom of God is ever lost. On the
contrary, it is multiplied and returned to us.... The
more we give, the more we will receive, not for our
own lusts or greedy desires, but so we can seek His
Kingdom even more, and help others to do so as well."*

Have you ever felt that you had given up something
for the Kingdom of God and felt it was lost? Have
you ever seen something you thought was lost re-
stored? Have you been able to use this to help others?

The Divine Priority Mandate

Do not be afraid, little flock, for your Father has been pleased to give you the kingdom (Luke 12:32).

TODAY'S DEVOTION

Our first priority—the principal and most important activity of our life—is to seek the Kingdom of God. But how do we do that? What does it mean to seek God's Kingdom? How can we find the Kingdom of God if we don't know how to look for it or what to look for? God will never demand from us what He does not supply. He will never instruct us to do something that He doesn't show us how to do.

Even more important, He wants us to seek and find His Kingdom. He gave us this promise: "You will seek Me and find Me when you seek Me with all your heart" (Jer. 29:13). Finding God is the same as finding His Kingdom because the two are inseparable.

A mandate is a command issued by a ruler. Jesus' charge to us to seek first the Kingdom and righteousness of God is a command, not a suggestion. If we claim to be His followers and call Him Lord, we must obey Him. Otherwise, He is not our Lord, and we will never find the Kingdom and never experience the fulfillment of our life purpose.

(Excerpt: *Applying the Kingdom*, Chapter 4)

QUESTIONS

1. How do we seek the Kingdom of God? What does it mean to seek God's Kingdom? How can we find the Kingdom of God if we don't know how to look for it or what to look for? What has God taught you about the Kingdom?

2. Explain what Jeremiah 29:13 means to you. How does finding God mean that you have found the Kingdom?

3. What are some New Testament commands that Jesus gave us? Why do many Christians respond to these commands as if they were suggestions?

4. In the Kingdom of God, obedience is not optional. What does this statement tell you about the kind of government that exists in the Kingdom of God? Do you embrace God's commands with immediate and joyful obedience?

5. How does obedience affect our ability to experience the Kingdom of God? What does lack of obedience do to cloud our minds and hearts toward God's priorities?

MEDITATION

"Only those who seek the Kingdom of God will find it, and with the seeking comes the understanding of the Kingdom and how it operates. Jesus told His closest followers, 'The knowledge of the secrets of the kingdom of heaven has been given to you...' (Matt. 13:11a). When we understand how the Kingdom operates, we will understand how to live in the Kingdom and experience its fullness in our lives."

Are you experiencing the fullness of the Kingdom in your life? Are there areas that you need to understand the secrets of the Kingdom so you can experience a greater degree of fullness. Be consistent in prayer to gain Kingdom secrets.

The Divine Command: "Seek"; The Divine Priority: "First"

B LESSED ARE THOSE WHO HUNGER AND THIRST FOR RIGHTEOUSNESS, FOR THEY WILL BE FILLED (MATTHEW 5:6).

TODAY'S DEVOTION

The divine command is to seek. To seek means to pursue the Kingdom with vigor and determination.

To seek also means to study.

Seeking also means to explore the Kingdom's power, its laws, its government, its culture, its society, its commands, its economy, its taxation—everything.

Another aspect of seeking is understanding. Once we understand, the promises of the Kingdom will begin manifesting in our lives.

To seek also means to learn, demonstrating the ability to perform the action learned, as well as to teach it to someone else.

If we desire to know the Kingdom and its ways, the King will make sure our desire is satisfied. Seeking the Kingdom is deliberate and proactive.

Finally, to seek the Kingdom means to become preoccupied with it. It possesses us.

The Divine Priority is that we must seek it first. Seeking the Kingdom first means that we pursue it as the principal thing, the first thing above and before and beyond all other things.

"Kingdom first!" does not mean first among many, but "first and only." Developing the habit of considering the Kingdom first will help you avoid a lot of mistakes and bad decisions.

(Excerpt: *Applying the Kingdom,* Chapter 4)

QUESTIONS

1. Do you pursue the Kingdom with vigor and determination? What characterizes this type of pursuit?

2. To seek means to study, understand, and learn. What are the differences between each of these? How well do you seek the Kingdom through these means?

3. In what ways have you explored the Kingdom? Are you on a path of discovery, or have you quit growing and learning about the Kingdom?

4. How well do you know Kingdom ways? Do others see evidence of Kingdom discoveries in your life?

5. How easy is it for you to seek the Kingdom of God first? "Kingdom first!" does not mean first among many, but "first and only." What does this mean to you?

MEDITATION

"Not only should we desire the Kingdom, but also we should have a passion for the Kingdom! What are you passionate about? What gets your blood going in the morning? What infuses your life with purpose? Everyone is passionate about something. If you are not passionate about the Kingdom of God, then you are focused on the wrong thing."

Think about your answers to these questions and pray through each one, asking the Lord to declare His passion toward you and how He wants you to reciprocate the passion toward Him.

The Divine Object: "The Kingdom of God"; The Divine Position: "God's Righteousness"

JESUS SAID, "BY THEIR FRUIT YOU WILL RECOGNIZE THEM. DO PEOPLE PICK GRAPES FROM THORN-BUSHES, OR FIGS FROM THISTLES? LIKEWISE EVERY GOOD TREE BEARS GOOD FRUIT, BUT A BAD TREE BEARS BAD FRUIT. A GOOD TREE CANNOT BEAR BAD FRUIT, AND A BAD TREE CANNOT BEAR GOOD FRUIT" (MATTHEW 7:16–18).

TODAY'S DEVOTION

The Kingdom is God's government. It is His rulership and dominion over Heaven and earth.

The word *Kingdom* also means "to have influence over a territory." When we seek first the Kingdom of God we are seeking His influence to be extended over the entire world in our private life, our business life, our marriage life, our relationships, our sexual life, and all other dimensions of life.

In the Kingdom of God we are under the administration of Heaven. This means that God, the King, becomes our reference point for everything. Our lives are supposed to manifest the fruit—the influence—of the Kingdom of God, so that anybody can look and tell where our allegiance lies.

We are also to seek His righteousness. This is not a first and second priority, but two parts of one complete whole. God's Kingdom cannot be separated from His righteousness. God is righteous; and, therefore, His Kingdom is also righteous.

God has committed Himself to you because you now are in right relationship with Him. To be righteous means that you are legal, lawful, in sync with the government. Stay in the law, and everything you need will come to you.

(Excerpt: *Applying the Kingdom*, Chapter 4)

QUESTIONS

1. Knowing that God's Kingdom is God's rulership should give you peace and security. Why? Knowing that He is King over both Heaven and earth should help Christians in what ways?

2. The Kingdom of God is over what territories of your life? What arenas in your personal life reflect His Kingdom the most? What areas reflect the Kingdom the least?

3. From your experience, what type of administration does the Kingdom of God have? How does the administration work for the world in general? How does the administration work for Kingdom citizens?

4. How easy is it for people to see your allegiance to the Kingdom? Are there any times when you have had to display this allegiance in a greater way in order to take a stand against unrighteousness?

5. How does righteousness make demands on your life? What things have you had to change in order to please the King of the Kingdom? How has Jesus' blood made you righteousness complete?

MEDITATION

"Only righteous people will enter the Kingdom.
The problem is that none of us are righteous on our own.
When we are born again, God imputes righteousness to us."

The word *righteous* is a legal term. It means "right positioning, to be in correct alignment with the ruling standard." Right standing carries with it the even deeper element of being in fellowship with that authority."

Give God praise for your righteous standing before Him. Thank Him for wanting to be in fellowship with you. Make time to fellowship with the Lord today.

The Power of Righteousness

I HAVE DONE WHAT IS RIGHTEOUS AND JUST; DO NOT LEAVE ME TO MY OPPRESSORS (PSALM 119:121).

TODAY'S DEVOTION

God's Kingdom and God's righteousness. Both are equally important and both are inseparable.

Righteousness is a legal word, not a religious word. Every country demands righteousness because righteousness simply means to be in conformity with the laws of the country.

In the Bible, righteousness almost always is linked in close proximity to justice, which means "rights." Righteousness is always related to justice because righteousness is a prerequisite for justice.

The Kingdom of God also has a constitution—the Bible. In a kingdom, the king's word is law. The citizens cannot debate it, challenge it, or change it. In the Kingdom of God, we stand either righteous or unrighteous with Kingdom law, the Word of God. It is a matter of positioning.

Righteousness means right positioning with the government. It is when a person takes up citizenship in a country and pledges to obey its laws. When Jesus said, "Seek first the kingdom of God and His righteousness," He was saying, "Seek to become a citizen of the Kingdom of God and then stay in alignment with the government's law. If you do those two things then everything you need will be added to you." What could be simpler?

(Excerpt: *Applying the Kingdom,* Chapter 14)

QUESTIONS

1. Explain why God's Kingdom and His righteousness are equally important. Why are they inseparable?

2. What does the word *righteousness* mean to you? How do we fulfill righteousness within a country?

3. What is the difference between righteousness and justice within the framework of God's Kingdom? How are righteousness and justice interconnected? Which one is dependent on the other being there first?

4. How does the constitution of a country define whether someone is righteous or unrighteous? How do we stand righteous before our King?

5. How does a citizen of the Kingdom of God stay in alignment with God's laws? How do you maintain your right standing before God?

MEDITATION

"One of humankind's greatest struggles is determining what is most important in life. The world offers a 'grab bag' of possibilities to choose from, but Jesus reduces the issues of life to two things: the Kingdom of God and the righteousness of God. Everything else in life is a byproduct.

"It is amazing how simple life becomes when you realize that you need to focus only on two things."

With so many choices in this world, how do you choose the best, the most important? How do you make sure that you are spending your life on the things that really count?

Two Priorities for Man

BUT YOU ARE A CHOSEN PEOPLE, A ROYAL PRIEST-HOOD, A HOLY NATION, A PEOPLE BELONGING TO GOD…(1 PETER 2:9A).

TODAY'S DEVOTION

There are two priorities for us: Kingdom and righteousness. Kingdom is the horizontal dimension that deals with power: rulership, dominion and control. It is kingship. Righteousness is the vertical dimension that deals with position: relationship, right standing, disposition, and authority. It is priesthood.

If you keep the vertical clear, the horizontal will be clear. If you are an effective priest, you will be an effective king. Kingdom makes you a citizen, but righteousness gives you access to all the rights, resources and privileges of citizenship.

Our two priorities are to seek Kingdom citizenship and the relationship that puts us in a position to demand things from the Kingdom. And the Kingdom government is responsible and obligated to the citizen. Righteousness gives us rights and rights activate the government to act on our behalf.

Let's summarize the relationship between kingdom and righteousness:

- Kingdom places us in citizenship; righteousness places in us relationship.
- Kingdom gives us rights to government benefits; righteousness gives us access to government benefits.
- Kingdom makes us legal; righteousness maintains our legal status.
- Righteousness is manifested in holiness.

Holiness is a manifestation of righteousness. Holiness is based on relationship, and relationship comes from righteousness.

(Excerpt: *Applying the Kingdom,* Chapter 5)

QUESTIONS

1. How does the horizontal work of the Kingdom and the vertical work of righteousness play out in your life? Do you see the intersection of both things within the Kingdom and within your life?

2. How effective are you as a priest of the Kingdom? How effective are you as a king? What can you do to increase your effectiveness in both roles?

3. What do you think about being in the position to demand things from the Kingdom? How do you feel about the Kingdom being obligated to you?

4. What rights do you have in the Kingdom? How well do you understand and exercise these rights?

5. Read over the four points summarizing the Kingdom and righteousness. Do you understand each point? Do you apply each point in your life experience?

MEDITATION

"If you get yourself out of alignment with the government, rights and privileges can be suspended, just as they are for citizens who are in prison for crimes they committed. They are still citizens but they no longer enjoy full rights and freedoms.

"This explains why many born-again Kingdom citizens struggle with basic needs from day to day and do not experience the fullness of Kingdom living. Righteousness is the key to abundant Kingdom living."

Are you taking proper care to stay in right standing with Kingdom government? Have you cut yourself off from access to the resources of Heaven because you have violated the laws and principles of the Kingdom?

Power Keys for Kingdom Life

FOR THE EYES OF THE LORD RANGE THROUGH-
OUT THE EARTH TO STRENGTHEN THOSE WHOSE
HEARTS ARE FULLY COMMITTED TO HIM (2 CHRONI-
CLES 16:9).

TODAY'S DEVOTION

Where does the power in righteousness come from? It comes from the King, who passes it down to us.

A scepter is the symbol of a king's royal authority. The scepter was a visible symbol of the king's power. When our King extends His scepter to us, we may enter and everything in the Kingdom becomes ours.

Here are seven more power keys. When you are in right standing with the King, the power of righteousness is:

1. *Governmental obligation.* The King is obligated to take care of your life.

2. *Governmental protection.* The King is obligated to protect you.

3. *Governmental support.* The King is obligated to support your life, to uphold you in everything.

4. *Governmental provisions.* The King provides you with everything you need.

5. *Governmental commitment.* The King is committed to take care of you.

6. *Governmental responsibility.* When you are under the King's authority, the King has a place of responsibility toward you.

7. *Righteousness activates the government.* You activate the entire machine of the government. God's eyes are on the righteous. Our righteousness activates the government. His own nature and promises obligate Him to act.

What a powerful list!

(Excerpt: *Applying the Kingdom,* Chapter 5)

QUESTIONS

1. How does it feel to know that if you are in right standing with the King, He extends His scepter to you? What does this mean for your life?

2. How has the authority of God been expressed in your life? How has the power of God been expressed in your life? How does acceptance from the King make both the authority and the power of God available to you?

3. How does the power of righteousness work for you in terms of governmental obligation toward you? How does the power of righteousness work in your life with regard to governmental protection?

4. How does the power of righteousness work for you in terms of governmental support toward you? How does the power of righteousness work in your life with regard to governmental provision?

5. How does the power of righteousness work for you in terms of governmental commitment toward you? How does the power of righteousness work in your life with regard to governmental commitment? How does righteousness activate the government of God in your life?

MEDITATION

"Our authority in the Kingdom of God is righteousness. As long as we stay lined up with the government's laws, we have power with the government. God gives us power to ask for anything we need.

"The foundation for our exercising the authority of God is our relationship with God. Once we are lined up with God, He will lavish His faithfulness and love upon us. Talk about getting your needs met!"

Can you believe that if you are in the right position with the King, He wants to overload you with blessings? Thank Him for the provision, but also the means to that provision in your life.

Constitutional Principles for the Pursuit of Righteousness

THE RIGHTEOUSNESS OF THE UPRIGHT DELIVERS THEM, BUT THE UNFAITHFUL ARE TRAPPED BY EVIL DESIRES (PROVERBS 11:6).

TODAY'S DEVOTION

If you want to understand the principles under which a nation or a kingdom operates, you examine its constitution, the Bible.

Wealth is worthless in the day of wrath, but righteousness delivers from death (Proverbs 11:4).

Do you want long life? Then live for righteousness. Righteousness is its own reward. Righteousness brings reward and the link between the two is obedience. The pursuit of righteousness is the fundamental operating principle for citizens of the Kingdom of God.

Righteousness exalts a nation, but sin is a disgrace to any people (Proverbs 14:34).

Righteousness is not only personal but also corporate.

...with righteousness He will judge the needy, with justice He will give decisions for the poor of the earth (Isaiah 11:4).

This verse says that poverty is solved by righteousness.

For the kingdom of God is not a matter of eating and drinking, but of righteousness, peace and joy in the Holy Spirit (Romans 14:17).

The Kingdom of God operates on righteousness. Righteousness is the scepter of God's throne. Righteousness guarantees that we will receive all the rights that are ours under Kingdom law. And its results are treasures the world craves: peace, quietness, confidence—and joy unspeakable.

(Excerpt: *Applying the Kingdom,* Chapter 5)

QUESTIONS

Look at the Scriptures on the previous page and fill in the chart below.

Scripture	Benefits of Righteousness	Righteousness Has Benefitted Me in This Way...
Proverbs 11:4		
Proverbs 14:34		
Isaiah 11:4		
Romans 14:17		

MEDITATION

"In every nation today there is a crying need for righteous Kingdom citizens to be active in the political arena, not only as voters but also as candidates and office holders. The only way for justice to prevail is for that nation to be governed by God's principles of righteousness. The only way for righteousness to govern a nation is for righteous citizens to wield their influence and example at every level of government."

What is your political life like? Are you involved to the extent that God has asked you to be personally? So you vote? Do you speak out to the elected officials about issues that affect the righteousness of the nation? What does God want you to do in terms of political activism?

Righteous Positioning: The Key to Abundant Kingdom Living

As the deer pants for streams of water, so my soul pants for you, O God. My soul thirsts for God, for the living God. When can I go and meet with God? (Psalm 42:1-2)

TODAY'S DEVOTION

For many believers today a great disconnect exists between the promises of the Kingdom and the personal realities of daily experience. We are neck-deep in debt and always seem to end up with too much month left at the end of the money.

As long as we pursue things, we will never know true peace, contentment, or joy. Somehow we must be delivered from our slavery to things. Deliverance is found in only one place: in pursuit of the Kingdom and righteousness of God.

It is a matter of exchanging one hunger for another. Our hunger for things will never be satisfied. But Jesus said, "Blessed are those who hunger and thirst for righteousness, for they will be filled" (Matt. 5:6). How hungry are you? What are you hungry for? Is your hunger for the Kingdom greater than your hunger for things? Do you thirst for righteousness more than you thirst for material prosperity? King David of Israel wrote, "Delight yourself in the Lord and He will give you the desires of your heart" (Ps. 37:4). If the Kingdom and righteousness of God are your chief desire and delight, He will take care of everything else.

(Excerpt: *Applying the Kingdom,* Chapter 6)

QUESTIONS

1. Why do you think "many believers today [have] a great disconnect exists between the promises of the Kingdom and the personal realities of daily experience"? Is this true in your life?

2. Do you find you have too much month at the end of the money? Are you in debt? Why are most people in debt? How does debt show the disposition toward things?

3. How does our pursuit of things rob us of peace, contentment, or joy? Why do we need deliverance to rid us of this pursuit? Where is the only place to receive this deliverance? Why?

4. How is it possible to exchange one hunger for another? If we exchange our hunger of things for the hunger of righteousness, what will we receive?

5. Explain what Psalm 37:4 means to you? Have you experienced the truth of this Scripture in your own life?

MEDITATION

"Imagine being stranded in the desert under the baking sun without food or water. After a couple of days, the only thing on your mind is the desire to satisfy your hunger and thirst. You are willing to sacrifice anything, part with anything, do anything to fill the greatest craving in your heart. Jesus said that this is the kind of all-consuming desire you should have for the Kingdom and righteousness of God."

How singularly focused are you toward your God? How thirsty are you for His presence? How hungry are you for His Word?

The Divine Disposition

IF I REGARD INIQUITY IN MY HEART, THE LORD I WILL NOT HEAR (PSALM 66:18 NKJV).

TODAY'S DEVOTION

A continuing hunger and thirst for righteousness positions us to enter into the fullness of Kingdom life. Our pursuit of righteousness places us in the right positioning to receive all the rights, resources, blessings, and privileges of the Kingdom that are ours as Kingdom citizens.

It is a very simple dynamic. As long as we obey the law, we have access. As soon as we disobey, that access shuts down. This explains why so many believers struggle, pinching pennies, trying to make ends meet but never seem to have enough, with no peace, joy, or contentment. They are out of alignment with their government and their access to Kingdom resources has been shut off.

Whenever this happens, it is always due to sin. Sin interrupts our communication with God and shuts down the flow of His resources to us. Iniquity refers specifically to invisible sin, such as greed, envy, lust, and hatred, and is worse than physical sin. Invisible sin gives rise to visible sins of action.

But we must choose the path of righteousness and be in the right positioning with regard to our King's requirements. We must be in the position to receive His favor.

(Excerpt: *Applying the Kingdom*, Chapter 6)

QUESTIONS

1. What does the "fullness of Kingdom life" mean to you? How do you enter into this fullness? This seems so simple; why do we find this process do difficult?

2. What do you think are the "rights, resources, blessings, and privileges of the Kingdom that are ours as Kingdom citizens"? What have you personally experienced in each of these categories?

3. Why do you think obedience is so tied up with receiving access to the Kingdom's benefits? Do you think this means that we must have perfect obedience to obtain any of these benefits? Why or why not?

4. How does the way we live our lives show how aligned we are to the Kingdom of God? How do we ultimately demonstrate on a daily basis whether we are pursuing righteousness or pursuing something else?

5. How does sin work within your life to display your disobedience? How does iniquity manifest itself in sin? How does a pursuit of righteousness help us get on the path of obedience?

MEDITATION

"Purity of heart is a critical, indispensable key to abundant Kingdom life. Jesus said, 'Blessed are the pure in heart, for they will see God' (Matt. 5:8). Literally, this means that the pure in heart will see God in everything. If our minds are pure, we will see God in everything and in everyone. This is the answer to the problem of greed, lust, jealousy, or any kind of impure or improper thought or attitude."

Do you think you are pure in heart for the most part? How much do you see God in everything?

The Fruit of Righteousness

FOR THE LORD loves the just and will not forsake His faithful ones. They will be protected forever, but the offspring of the wicked will be cut off; the righteous will inherit the land and dwell in it forever (PSALM 37:28-29).

TODAY'S DEVOTION

Righteousness bears abundant fruit in our lives. One of these is a spirit of generosity, along with the means and capacity to give generously. If we are heirs to the Kingdom of God and all its riches, which are infinite, we can give with no fear of running out.

The prosperity of the righteous is an ongoing blessing from God that spans generations. We should be so blessed that our children should inherit a multiplied blessing, because we lived our life rightly positioned with God's government.

Right positioning places us under the protection of the King, who will preserve us even when the wicked are destroyed.

The Bible is the constitution of the Kingdom of God and the source of righteousness for its citizens. If we don't know our constitution, we will not be able to obey it or claim our constitutional rights as Kingdom citizens.

The people of the world are looking for the Kingdom, but how will they learn of it if we keep silent? How we need today believing politicians and CEOs and managers and supervisors and employees who will stand up for righteousness.

Stand up for righteousness, and God will bless you with the whole Kingdom.

(Excerpt: *Applying the Kingdom,* Chapter 6)

QUESTIONS

1. Has righteous born abundant fruit in your life? How is righteousness connected to the fruit we bear?

2. How generous are you? Do you give from the perspective of what you can afford or from a position of what God desires? If He desires you to give more than what you have, what will He do in order to replenish your stores?

3. Why is the provision of an inheritance to future generations so important to the Kingdom of God? Are you in a position to leave an inheritance, materially, spiritually, emotionally, etc?

4. Do you feel well protected by your King? How can God punish the wicked and at the same time protect His Kingdom citizens while they live on the same planet?

5. How important do you think it is to tell about the Kingdom to the world? How do we communicate this? Are there ways beyond our words? What are you doing to let the world know about the Kingdom?

MEDITATION

*"If we are righteous, we will enjoy
the fruit of peace. Why? Because we are
not living for the pursuit of things anymore...*

*"Second, peace will produce the corollary effect
of quietness, or calm disposition, even in trouble...*

*"Third, peace also produces confidence—total trust
and faith in the care, provision, and protection
of God's government. This means that we can go
to sleep at night free of worry, fear, and uncertainty."*

Does an absence of frustration and worry describe your life? Are you at peace? Do you have a calm, quiet disposition no matter what happens? Do you have confidence in the protection of God's government on an ongoing basis?

Positioning Is Essential for Kingdom Life

FOR IN THE GOSPEL A RIGHTEOUSNESS FROM GOD IS REVEALED, A RIGHTEOUSNESS THAT IS BY FAITH FROM FIRST TO LAST, JUST AS IT IS WRITTEN: "THE RIGHTEOUS WILL LIVE BY FAITH" (ROMANS 1:17).

TODAY'S DEVOTION

Positioning places us under proper authority in the Kingdom. Even Jesus had to get into position [through baptism] before He began public ministry.

But John tried to deter Him, saying, "I need to be baptized by You, and do You come to me?" Jesus replied, "Let it be so now; it is proper for us to do this to fulfill all righteousness." Then John consented (Matthew 3:14-15).

In essence, Jesus was saying, "This is not a matter of greatness, but a matter of positioning. I have to get under you in order for Me to be under Myself."

If Jesus Christ had to submit to the authority He established, who are we to think that we don't? Our protection is submission to Kingdom authority, positioning ourselves in alignment to the Word and will of the King.

As soon as Jesus was baptized, Heaven opened, and the Spirit descended like a dove. A voice said, "This is My Son, whom, I love; with Him I am well pleased" (Matt. 3:16-17).

Righteousness is pleasing to God, and righteousness means positioning ourselves under His authority.

Righteous positioning, which is based on obedience, is so important that it is the standard of measure in the Kingdom.

(Excerpt: *Applying the Kingdom,* Chapter 6)

QUESTIONS

1. How does "positioning place us under proper authority in the King-dom"? Do you feel you are in the position that puts you under the proper authority in the Kingdom? Why or why not?

2. Why did Jesus choose to be under earthly authority when He didn't have to do so? What do you learn from His example?

3. Explain the difference between greatness and position, according to Jesus' reply to John. How does this clarify how we should treat greatness?

4. How does submitting to Kingdom authority protect us? What are some ways in which you have received protection when you have submitted to Kingdom authority?

5. How are righteousness, obedience, and positioning connected? What testimony do you have of these three and how they have worked in your life?

MEDITATION

"Christ is the end of the law. For everyone who believes—everyone who trusts and submits their lives to Him—Jesus becomes their righteousness.

"The righteousness we receive in Christ is not for ourselves alone. He commissions us to spread the word of His righteousness to others so they too may become rightly positioned with Him. This commission is called the ministry of reconciliation. This is the good news of the Kingdom!"

Do you regularly thank God for the righteousness you have in Jesus? Do you see your righteousness as a means to help others receive the same righteousness? Pray about whom you can share the good news of the Kingdom with today.

Positioning From a Kingdom Perspective

BUT HIS DELIGHT IS IN THE LAW OF THE LORD, AND ON HIS LAW HE MEDITATES DAY AND NIGHT. HE IS LIKE A TREE PLANTED BY STREAMS OF WATER, WHICH YIELDS ITS FRUIT IN SEASON AND WHOSE LEAF DOES NOT WITHER. WHATEVER HE DOES PROSPERS (PSALM 1:2-3).

TODAY'S DEVOTION

What good does it do to try to live right and do the right thing? If righteousness is so important, why do the wicked prosper?

Asaph was so troubled over this he almost abandoned his attempt to live righteously, until he received a revelation from God. When he began to see things from the vantage point of the Kingdom of Heaven, his entire perspective changed:

> *When I tried to understand all this, it was oppressive to me till I entered the sanctuary of God; then I understood their final destiny. Surely you place them on slippery ground; you cast them down to ruin. How suddenly they are destroyed, completely swept away by terrors! As a dream when one awakes, so when you arise, O Lord, you will despise them as fantasies* (Psalm 73:16-20).

Things look different when viewed from a Kingdom perspective.

So what good is righteousness? It gives us true stability, success, health, wealth that lasts, and positions us to overcome all of life's troubles.

Even though the righteousness we receive in Christ is not given for us alone but also for the purpose of the ministry of reconciliation, righteousness does bring with it significant personal benefits.

(Excerpt: *Applying the Kingdom,* Chapter 7)

QUESTIONS

1. Have you ever questioned why the wicked seem to prosper? Have you ever wondered about the value of righteousness in your life?

2. What was different about Asaph's perspective about the righteous and the unrighteous as given to us in Psalm 73? What about your perspective? Does it need to be changed so you can understand this principle of the Kingdom?

3. Explain the benefits of righteousness to citizens of the Kingdom. What are earthly benefits? What are the Heavenly benefits?

4. How well do you promote the Kingdom's earthly benefits to others by the way in which you live your life? In what ways could you improve?

5. How well do you promote the Kingdom's eternal benefits to others by the way in which you live your life? In what ways could you improve?

MEDITATION

*"Whenever we sow seeds of generosity
we are setting ourselves up for a harvest
of greater righteousness and prosperity.*

*"Everything God gives you is a seed. Sow your
seed faithfully, and God will replace it with even
more seed so you can increase your generosity.
And He will continue to do so, as long as you
use what He gives for His sake and for the
sake of others rather than for your own sake."*

What seeds has God given to you that you need to sow? How faithful have you been in sowing them? What increases of seed have you experienced?

The Benefit of the King's Favor

... Your throne, O God, will last forever and ever, and righteousness will be the scepter of Your kingdom (Hebrews 1:8).

TODAY'S DEVOTION

Righteousness attracts God because He is righteous. He looks favorably on all who seek to live righteously in faith. Just as people in earthly kingdoms long for the favor of their king, so we too should seek the favor of the King of Heaven. We should look for Him to extend His scepter over us.

None could enter the king's presence unless he first extended his scepter to them. If a king wants to show you favor, he will extend his scepter over you, and the next thing he says becomes law over you. What you were or what you are now does not matter. All that matters is what the king says right now. He gives because he wants to; that's why it is called favor.

Traditionally, a king would hold his scepter in his right hand. The Bible uses similar imagery to refer to God as King. Those under God's favor are said to be at His right hand, while those under His judgment are at His left. If the right hand of the Lord is upon you, it means that He has appointed His authority toward you; He has given you access.

(Excerpt: *Applying the Kingdom*, Chapter 7)

QUESTIONS

1. How does righteousness attract God? Why? When you are righteous, have you felt the Lord close by?

2. Is there someone on earth of whom you have tried to seek favor, either in your past or present? Why did you want his or her favor? Why should we desire God's favor?

3. Why is God's scepter so important to the government of the Kingdom? What does it express about God's role and nature? What does it mean to us as Kingdom citizens?

4. Why is it smarter for us to wait for the King's scepter to be extended to us than for us to work for a lifetime in our own effort? What does scepter mean to our efforts?

5. How does God's scepter grant us access to His presence? How does His scepter grant us His favor and all the other attributes of His character?

MEDITATION

"If you line yourself up with God in righteousness, He will extend His scepter, He will direct His favor toward you. Authority is better than work.

"Jesus told us to seek first God's Kingdom and His righteousness and everything would be added to us. Righteousness must come before addition. But when God has decided to add the addition to you, nothing in Heaven or on earth will keep Him from giving it to you."

How have you experienced God's favor? Has addition come to you because of righteousness? Are these things you can acknowledge easily?

The Benefits of Understanding and Discernment, Protection and Promotion

ANYONE WHO LIVES ON MILK, BEING STILL AN INFANT, IS NOT ACQUAINTED WITH THE TEACHING ABOUT RIGHTEOUSNESS. BUT SOLID FOOD IS FOR THE MATURE, WHO BY CONSTANT USE HAVE TRAINED THEMSELVES TO DISTINGUISH GOOD FROM EVIL (HEBREWS 5:13-14).

TODAY'S DEVOTION

The pursuit of righteousness is the secret to maturity, understanding, and discernment in Kingdom living. Lack of righteousness in our lives leads to misalignment with God and stunts our growth so that we never progress beyond the stage of spiritual toddlers. Only those committed to righteousness will reach maturity.

When we actively pursue righteousness, we enjoy security and protection. Under God's protection and favor He enables us to overcome every obstacle and meet every challenge so that we live life to the fullest.

This is the confidence we have in approaching God: that if we ask anything according to His will, He hears us. And if we know that He hears us—whatever we ask—we know that we have what we have asked of Him (1 John 5:14-15).

Asking "according to His will" means not only agreeing with God's will but also asking from the place of righteous positioning, because righteousness is always God's will. This is perhaps one of the most important reasons of all for us to be careful to do nothing that will bring us out of alignment with God and interfere with our relationship with Him.

(Excerpt: *Applying the Kingdom,* Chapter 7)

QUESTIONS

1. How has God grown you from that of a baby Christian to continued maturity? How does righteousness play a part in this growth?

2. What security and protection have you received from God? Have you received promotion from the King of the Kingdom?

3. How are protection and promotion related? How would you explain this relationship in terms of your own life's experience?

4. Explain 1 John 5:14-15 and its effect on your prayer life. How do you know if you have met the prerequisites for answered prayer?

5. How does righteousness demonstrate God's will? Is there any possible way God's will would not be involved in answers to prayer?

MEDITATION

*"We often have little or no control over what
comes into our lives or how people act toward us
but we always have control over how we respond.
Keeping our pipeline clear is up to us; God will
not do it for us. He will not force us to live
righteously. But unless we do, we will never experience
the benefits and blessings that righteousness brings."*

How does this principle keep us from having a "victim" mentality and understand our challenges in light of the God's blessings?

The Benefits of Deliverance and Prosperity

THE RIGHTEOUS WILL FLOURISH LIKE A PALM TREE, THEY WILL GROW LIKE A CEDAR OF LEBANON; PLANTED IN THE HOUSE OF THE LORD, THEY WILL FLOURISH IN THE COURTS OF OUR GOD. THEY WILL STILL BEAR FRUIT IN OLD AGE, THEY WILL STAY FRESH AND GREEN, PROCLAIMING, "THE LORD IS UPRIGHT; HE IS MY ROCK, AND THERE IS NO WICKEDNESS IN HIM" (PSALM 92:12-15).

TODAY'S DEVOTION

As long as we are aligned with God, He will deliver us from all our troubles. This does not mean that we will never experience trouble in life, but it does mean that we can trust God to carry us through and give us the strength and the grace to prevail.

Righteousness is a fundamental part of the solid foundation on which we must build our lives if we are to withstand the storm.

Righteousness is also the key to prosperity.

Misfortune pursues the sinner, but prosperity is the reward of the righteous. A good man leaves an inheritance for his children's children, but a sinner's wealth is stored up for the righteous (Proverbs 13:21-22).

The life of the righteous will be full, abundant, and fruitful in every sense and in every dimension. In contrast, sinners (the unrighteous) will face misfortune after misfortune.

Unlike the unrighteous, who will wither and be blown away like chaff in the wind, the righteous will flourish and remain fruitful for a lifetime. Our witness to the greatness and righteousness of God should be just as strong, and even stronger, at the end of our days as at any other time in life.

(Excerpt: *Applying the Kingdom*, Chapter 7)

QUESTIONS

1. Have you ever experienced the deliverance of God during a particularly challenging time? How did God's deliverance show itself? Why do you think God provided this deliverance?

2. How are righteousness and deliverance connected? In what way does righteousness keep us in the position to receive God's deliverance?

3. What is the connection between righteousness and prosperity? How can we keep from seeking prosperity instead of righteousness? How should we be expectant of prosperity?

4. Have you experienced the following to be true? "The life of the righteous will be full, abundant, and fruitful in every sense and in every dimension." What does this say about our faith in our King?

5. Why are we to produce fruit throughout our lives until the day we die? How does this demonstrate the mission assignment that God has for each one of us in His Kingdom on earth?

MEDITATION

*"In the Kingdom of God, righteousness is
the plumb line God uses to measure whether
our lives are 'true to plumb' or out of alignment.*

*"The Kingdom of God has everything we could
ever possibly need or want; but our lives must be
true to plumb. Being born again is the first step because
it gets us into the Kingdom, but our access to Kingdom
resources grows as we grow in practical righteousness."*

How do you measure up? If God dropped His plumb line alongside your life today, where would you fall? Would your life be out of alignment or would you be true to plumb?

The Kingdom Key to Accessing the Keys of the Kingdom

THE BLESSING OF THE LORD BRINGS WEALTH, AND HE ADDS NO TROUBLE TO IT (PROVERBS 10:22).

TODAY'S DEVOTION

The concept of the Kingdom of Heaven calls for a complete change of thinking. Moving from a worldly view to a Kingdom view requires a total paradigm shift. Priorities in the Kingdom are different from those in the world. Worth and value are assigned differently. Many of the things the world values most are regarded as worthless in the Kingdom of Heaven. Standards for evaluating greatness are very different between the world and the Kingdom. The world judges greatness in terms of money, power, and influence, while the Kingdom sees it in humility and self-giving service. And finally, the Kingdom and the world take entirely different views from each other with regard to things.

All human religions are built on the promise of things: a good harvest, the favor of the gods, victory over one's enemies, good health, great wealth, enlightenment, control or manipulation of the environment. "Religious" Christians are the same way, except that they rely on Jesus to provide what they want.

Prosperity without pressure! Wealth without worry! Treasure without trouble! These are the realities when we live on Kingdom land and abide by the laws of the King who owns it all.

(Excerpt: *Applying the Kingdom,* Chapter 8)

QUESTIONS

The author contrasts the Kingdom of Heaven with a worldly view of life. Use the chart to contrast these two mindsets and note what you need to implement in your own life. We have entered the first row to get you started.

Concept	The Kingdom of Heaven	The World	Personal Notes for My Life
Ways of Thinking	God's perspective	Political correctness	Check where I bought into the world's way of thinking
Paradigm shift			
Priorities			
Worth and Value			
Standards of evaluating greatness			
Material things			
Religion			
Prosperity, wealth and treasure			

MEDITATION

"The lure of things is so powerful that even many Kingdom citizens who once were serious about their walk with God and their righteous positioning have been seduced by it. Once they could be seen at the church building every time the doors were open, at worship, at prayer meetings, at Bible study, participating in ministry projects. Now, they are almost never around. When you ask them why, they are always ready with an excuse."

Do you find these statements to be true about some people you know? Have you ever made up excuses for a lack of participation in the things of the Kingdom? Are you buying into any excuses today?

Determining Your Net Worth

LOOK AT THE BIRDS OF THE AIR; THEY DO NOT
SOW OR REAP OR STORE AWAY IN BARNS, AND
YET YOUR HEAVENLY FATHER FEEDS THEM. ARE YOU
NOT MUCH MORE VALUABLE THAN THEY? (MATTHEW
6:26)

TODAY'S DEVOTION

We are of priceless worth to God irregardless of any possessions we own. Jesus used the example of the birds and how God feeds them even though they do not "sow or reap or store away in barns" (Matt. 6:26). Then Jesus asks, "Are you not much more valuable than they?" Our innate importance attracts things. God does not give us things to make us important but because we are important.

Every human desires things. This is a God-given, and therefore godly, desire. What is ungodly is pursuing things as gods. God wants us to have them but He also wants to show us how to acquire them in the right way and with the proper spirit.

This is one of the main reasons why many born-again believers who are caught up in a religious mind-set do not see the benefits and prosperity and fruitfulness of the Kingdom manifesting in their lives. They approach the whole matter of Kingdom access as supplicants with pleas rather than as citizens with rights.

Access to the things of Heaven requires the correct keys; knowledge and application of the correct principles that will release them.

(Excerpt: *Applying the Kingdom*, Chapter 8)

QUESTIONS

1. How does the world determine your net worth? How does the Kingdom of God determine your net worth? How does your value fluctuate in the world but remain constant in the Kingdom?

2. Think through all the different ways in which God cares for birds. How significant are birds in the animal kingdom? Does this help us understand the full spectrum of care God has provided for us?

3. Is the desire for things ungodly? In what context are we to ask for things? What perspective are we to have toward material things we desire?

4. How does a religious mind-set regard material things? How does someone with a religious mind-set pray for things? How are Kingdom citizens supposed to receive material things?

5. When we exercise our Kingdom rights to ask the King for things, what needs to be in place? What do we need to understand before we can have access to the resources of the Kingdom?

MEDITATION

*"The pursuit of things in a kingdom not only shows
distrust but is also an insult to the king. It shows
distrust by questioning the king's motives and intentions.
It insults the king by questioning his ability. One of the
keys to accessing the things of the Kingdom is coming to the
place where we are completely confident that God possesses
both the ability and the desire to supply everything we need."*

Have you been caught up in the pursuit of things at
any time in your life? Did you realize you were dis-
trusting and insulting your King? Confess and repent
of any way you have not given your trust fully to the
King of the Kingdom.

The Divine Obligation

H IS DIVINE POWER HAS GIVEN US EVERYTHING WE NEED FOR LIFE AND GODLINESS THROUGH OUR KNOWLEDGE OF HIM WHO CALLED US BY HIS OWN GLORY AND GOODNESS (2 PETER 1:3).

TODAY'S DEVOTION

The access keys to Kingdom things are the pursuit of the Kingdom of God and His righteousness. Seek these two things, Jesus said, and all the other things—the things of the Kingdom—would be added.

- All your physical needs—food, drink, clothing, car, housing, health.

- All your social needs—all your relationships. God will add the right people in your life.

- All your emotional needs—peace and a calm and tranquil spirit for every situation.

- All your psychological needs—stability. He will give you the grace to avoid becoming stressed out and burned out.

- All your financial needs—wealth. This includes both spiritual and material wealth, both the tangible and the intangible, the visible and the invisible.

- All your security needs—protection. God protects and over-shadows the righteous.

- All of your needs for self-significance—value.

- All your sense of purpose—vision. Instead of focusing on things you will once more focus on your assignment and move toward your destiny.

All these things will be added to you when you apply the keys of a whole-hearted seeking of the Kingdom and righteousness of God. What a way to live!

(Excerpt: *Applying the Kingdom,* Chapter 8)

QUESTIONS

Think through all the other things of the Kingdom and personalize each one.

Things of the Kingdom	What I am in need of today
Physical needs	
Social needs	
Emotional needs	
Psychological needs	
Financial needs	
Security needs	
Self-significance	
Purpose	

MEDITATION

"The secret key to Kingdom things is position and disposition. Disposition is Kingdom citizenship. Position is righteousness. Position and disposition: those are the keys. Get your citizenship in order and then stay in right relationship with the heavenly country and all these things will be added to you. Things are not blessings. They are by-products of Kingdom citizenship."

Are you in the position and disposition for Kingdom things? Are you ready to receive the by-products of your Kingdom citizenship?

The Answer to Human Motivation

YOU WILL AGAIN OBEY THE LORD AND FOLLOW ALL HIS COMMANDS I AM GIVING YOU TODAY. THEN THE LORD YOUR GOD WILL MAKE YOU MOST PROSPEROUS IN ALL THE WORK OF YOUR HANDS AND IN THE FRUIT OF YOUR WOMB, THE YOUNG OF YOUR LIVESTOCK AND THE CROPS OF YOUR LAND? (DEUTERONOMY 30:8-9)

TODAY'S DEVOTION

Blessings and provision are a real, natural, and vital part of Kingdom life, but if we are not careful we will end up making them the object of our faith rather than its natural by-product.

The Kingdom principle of addition operates on obedience: faithful observance of Kingdom law and clean living.

We cannot expect God to add things to us if we are living in sin. That is why many of us fret and sweat just to pay our bills every month. We're not living right. Our lives are out of alignment with God's government. The rewards of the Kingdom on God's part require right living on our part.

Worship alone is not enough. Neither is praying. Right living means making a deliberate, clean break with sin, accompanied by confession if necessary, and a resolute, careful determination to live every day in obedience to the laws of God. It means laying aside dishonesty, immorality, coarse or foul language, gossip, slander, backbiting, backstabbing, envy, jealousy, pride, selfish ambition, and lying. Right living means taking up a humble spirit of submission and service to God in which we first love God with all our heart and then love our neighbor as ourselves.

(Excerpt: *Applying the Kingdom,* Chapter 9)

QUESTIONS

1. How do you think Kingdom citizens can avoid making material things the object of our faith? How can we keep our focus on the Kingdom and let material things be the by-product of our faith?

2. How is obedience tied to the principle of Kingdom addition? How is our obedience expressed?

3. How does living in sin affect the way we handle our monthly bills and the ability to pay them?

4. What "religious" things do we use to try to earn our access to God's resources? How do these things fail to show righteous living on our part?

5. What should be the focus of our worship or tithing or good works? What do we need to keep us focused on the King and His righteousness and not on the by-products of the Kingdom?

MEDITATION

"The Kingdom is not a tool for us to use to get things from God. That is not the purpose of the Kingdom. Most of the people in our modern, consumer-driven culture…[have an] unremitting obsession with things they are perpetually tired, distracted, depressed, irritable and, if not sick already, prime candidates for stress- and anxiety-induced illness. The pursuit of things is detrimental to our health."

How can the pursuit of things affect your personality and character? How can it affect your health? Have you ever seen this to be true in your life?

The Divine Strategy for Provision

THE LORD WILL AGAIN DELIGHT IN YOU AND MAKE YOU PROSPEROUS, JUST AS HE DELIGHTED IN YOUR FATHERS, IF YOU OBEY THE LORD YOUR GOD AND KEEP HIS COMMANDS AND DECREES THAT ARE WRITTEN IN THIS BOOK OF THE LAW AND TURN TO THE LORD YOUR GOD WITH ALL YOUR HEART AND WITH ALL YOUR SOUL (DEUTERONOMY 30:9B–10).

TODAY'S DEVOTION

God wants to give you the desires of your heart. As a matter of fact, He wants to fulfill your highest dreams because He is the one who put those dreams in your heart. What He does not want is for you to put your dreams and desires ahead of Him. That's why Jesus says that all these things will be added to you.

When God adds to your life it means:

1. Things will be attracted to you.

2. Things will find you.

3. Things will come to your life.

4. Things will come without stress.

5. Things will be given as a favor and reward, like a gift, not as something you earned.

6. Things will come without struggle.

7. Things will be seen as natural.

8. Things will be given to you as needed.

9. Things will not be pursued. If you are pursuing the Kingdom and righteousness, you won't have time to pursue other things as your highest priority. That's why God will give them to you.

10. Things will not be your source. Things are commodities, tools, resources to be used to advance God's Kingdom on earth. God is your source. Look to Him.

(Excerpt: *Applying the Kingdom,* Chapter 9)

QUESTIONS

1. Things may not seem like they are our focus, but an analysis of your time, energy, and tears may be revealing. What do these reveal about you?

2. Have you ever felt things were attracted to you like a magnet? Have you sensed that things unexpectedly found you, coming into your life at "just the right time"? Did you see these kinds of events as the hand of God supplying your needs?

3. Have you ever experienced blessings that came to you without your earning them? Have you ever received something that came without struggle or stress? Have you praised God for these blessings?

4. Have you experienced the provision of God in a way that gave you what you needed, not more or less? Have you received something just when you needed it for an unexpected need? Do you trust that God will not give you what you should not have?

5. Is it easy for you to keep from pursuing things? Do you find contentment in what God provides for you? Do you see God as the Source of everything you have?

MEDITATION

"In order to unlock God's divine strategy for provision, we must first break out of our traditional mind-set that says that unless we labor, strive and concentrate all our energy on our daily needs, they will not be met. This does not mean that you don't work to support your family; it means that you don't obsess over it. You seek to obey God daily and trust Him to provide as He has promised."

Have you fallen into the trap of a traditional mind-set? How focused are you on your daily needs? Ask God to replace any wrong concepts with the release of His Kingdom principles.

The Addition Principle

GIVE US TODAY OUR DAILY BREAD (MATTHEW 6:11).

TODAY'S DEVOTION

The Kingdom principle of addition is founded on four significant truths that uniquely relate to the relationship that exists between the King and His citizens.

1. All that is needed for sustenance and life is the obligation of the king.

   A king is obligated to take care of his citizens because he owns everything and they will have nothing unless he gives it to them. Nobody is poor because nobody owns anything. All citizens have equal access to the king's assets.

2. Provisions for life are the responsibility of the king and not the citizen.

   I am not advising you to become irresponsible. It takes more responsibility to live in the Kingdom than to live in the world's system.

3. Kingdom favor is the unearned provision of the king.

   Favor is the system upon which the Kingdom of Heaven operates. Anything we work for constitutes earnings, not additions.

4. Man was never designed to pursue personal provisions, but the influence of Heaven on earth.

Our purpose is to spread the awareness and the influence of God's Kingdom throughout the earth. When we are about our Kingdom purpose, our King will supply all the provisions we need to do the job.

(Excerpt: *Applying the Kingdom,* Chapter 9)

QUESTIONS

1. How well do you understand that, as a citizen of the Kingdom, you do not own anything? Do you feel the obligation that the Lord has to take care of your needs?

2. How expectant are you toward the provision of your King? Do you labor for your earnings as part of His provision or because you are in control of your provision?

3. Do you regularly feel the favor of God? Are you experiencing the addition that is only in Him, rather than by the sweat of your brow?

4. How do you view the provisions that you do have? Do you see that they are part of the King's provision so that they might bring the influence of Heaven on earth?

5. How well do you see God's provision as a means for you to do your earthly assignment for His Kingdom? Are you about your Father's business?

MEDITATION

*"The 'Lord's Prayer' recorded in Matthew 6:9-13
contains only one phrase related to provision: 'Give
us today our daily bread' (Matt. 6:11). The real
focus of our prayers should be, 'Our Father in heaven,
hallowed be Your name, Your Kingdom come, Your will be
done on earth as it is in heaven' (Matt. 6:9-10). God's
desire is that we not live for things, but live for His influence."*

How much of your daily prayer time is focused on God and His Kingdom? How much of it has to do with your provision? Be sure to focus on the Source and not the sustenance.

Kingdom Provision and Purpose

Now it shall come to pass, if you diligently obey the voice of the Lord your God, to observe carefully all His commandments which I command you today, that the Lord your God will set you high above all nations of the earth. And all these blessings shall come upon you and overtake you, because you obey the voice of the Lord your God... (Deuteronomy 28:1-2 NKJV).

TODAY'S DEVOTION

Provision is a by-product of obedience. This kind of obedience involves much more than simple adherence to external rules or outward behavioral changes. You can obey on the outside and still possess a rebellious, disobedient heart. Isaiah records this complaint of God about His people: "The Lord says: 'These people come near to me with their mouth and honor me with their lips, but their hearts are far from me. Their worship of me is made up only of rules taught by men'" (Isa. 29:13). External obedience with a disobedient heart is not obedience at all.

Obedience that releases Kingdom provision begins in the heart and manifests in our outward lives. False external obedience is nothing more than a calculated ploy to manipulate God into giving us what we want, and it will fail every time. If we obey God's commands from our heart, the provisions of the Kingdom will overtake us.

In the Kingdom, assignment determines access. If you are committed to your Kingdom purpose, God will prosper you to whatever degree necessary for you to succeed. In the Kingdom, purpose attracts provision. Whenever a king makes an assignment, he makes full provision for its completion.

(Excerpt: *Applying the Kingdom*, Chapter 9)

QUESTIONS

1. How is provision a by-product of obedience? Has this been true in your own experience?

2. If God had spoken to you with the words from Isaiah 29:13, what reaction would you have had? Are any of these accusations true of your life? What do we need to do to keep from such an indictment?

3. Explain external obedience and heart disobedience and how they can exist at the same time. What can change a heart's attitude so that the internal and external match?

4. Where does Kingdom provision begin? How can we remind ourselves of this so that we stay focused on what our King wants, rather than what we want?

5. How does your Kingdom assignment determine your access to God's resources? How is your own purpose tied into God's provision? Relate this principle to your specific Kingdom assignment and purpose.

MEDITATION

"What is our purpose? To spread the knowledge and influence of the Kingdom of Heaven over all the earth. Success in such an assignment requires adequate daily provision. Man was created to work out his assignment, not work for a living. This doesn't mean we stop working; it means we change our reason for working."

Do you understand your purpose on earth? Take time to allow God to show you how He has positioned you for His glory and given you everything you need to be successful.

Service: The Heart of Kingdom Culture

B LESSED ARE THE POOR IN SPIRIT, FOR THEIRS IS THE KINGDOM OF HEAVEN (MATTHEW 5:3).

TODAY'S DEVOTION

God's intent for us as Kingdom citizens is that we take on the culture of Heaven so that in whatever we do or say it will be evident that we belong to the Kingdom of Heaven. As Kingdom citizens both our language and our lifestyle should reflect that.

The Kingdom of God is an actual country with its own government, laws, culture, and citizenry. Unlike earthly kingdoms, the Kingdom of Heaven is an eternal Kingdom.

God's Kingdom will endure from generation to generation. There is a place in the Kingdom for our children, and all other generations of our descendents until the end of time. If the Kingdom dies with us as far as our family is concerned, then we will have failed our King. God is always looking for more citizens for His Kingdom, and if we fail in our generation, who will introduce future generations to the Kingdom?

The enemy likes nothing more than to distract us into pursuing things because it keeps our attention away from the Kingdom and our Kingdom destiny. We must seek first the Kingdom and righteousness of God and trust Him to provide all the things that we need for daily life.

(Excerpt: *Applying the Kingdom*, Chapter 10)

QUESTIONS

1. How well do you model the culture of the Kingdom of God? How easy is it for people to see the Kingdom by how you live your life?

2. What are the differences that you know of between the Kingdom of Heaven and the kingdoms of the earth? How does the eternal nature of the Kingdom of Heaven give it a completely different dimension?

3. How well are you doing in demonstrating the Kingdom of Heaven within your family? Do you come from a heritage of Kingdom citizens? Are you a product of one of your ancestor's relationships with God?

4. Are you providing a legacy for the next generation? Are there Kingdom citizens following in your footsteps?

5. How does the pursuit of things distract us from producing the generational legacy we are supposed to produce? How can we keep from this kind of distraction?

MEDITATION

"Jesus said, 'Blessed are the poor in spirit...'"
(Matt. 5:3). 'Poor in spirit' means 'spiritually
bankrupt, spiritually destitute and in great spiritual need.'
Jesus said that the Kingdom of Heaven is reserved for
those who recognize their spiritual poverty. If you are
spiritually empty, no religion, including institutionalized,
man-centered Christianity, can fill your emptiness. You will
never be satisfied until you receive the Kingdom."

Does "poor in spirit" describe you? Have you ever been in this state? How has the Kingdom been the answer to your spiritual bankruptcy?

The Culture of Servanthood

. . . Whoever wants to become great among you must be your servant, and whoever wants to be first must be your slave—just as the Son of Man did not come to be served but to serve, and to give His life as a ransom for many (Matthew 20:26b-28).

TODAY'S DEVOTION

Culture is the manifestation of the nature of the government in the lifestyle, customs, and morals of the people. When you enter the Kingdom of Heaven through the new birth in Christ, you become a Kingdom citizen and the culture of the Kingdom should begin to manifest in your life, your speech, and your behavior.

Kingdom culture is distinctly different from the cultures of any earthly country. The cultures of the world manifest an every-man- for-himself approach to life and success. Kingdom culture measures success by service and self-giving. Kingdom culture is a culture of servanthood.

If people are always calling on you or turning to you, that's a good sign. However, if you are the one they always avoid, perhaps it is time for you to reexamine your attitude, habits, and work ethic. If you do not have the spirit of service and hard work, it will not be only people avoiding you. Prosperity will avoid you as well.

Being a servant does not mean that you become subservient. It means that you find what you have and you give it to the world. That's what makes you great in the Kingdom of Heaven.

(Excerpt: *Applying the Kingdom,* Chapter 10)

QUESTIONS

1. What are some of the distinctives that make the Kingdom of Heaven different than any earthly kingdom? How are these a part of the culture of the Kingdom?

2. How do earthly kingdoms put pressure on its citizens for success? What does the Kingdom of Heaven do differently for its citizens?

3. What is a culture of servanthood? How does this culture manifest itself?

4. Are you a picture of servanthood? Do people see you as someone they can come to easily? Have you seen prosperity follow your service?

5. What is the difference from being servant-oriented and being subservient? Have you fallen into any traps of self-worth or self-criticism that made you feel subservient? How can we avoid these?

MEDITATION

"The presence of the Kingdom of Heaven on earth divides all the people on earth into two groups: those who are Kingdom citizens and those who are not. This is a critical distinction. Our purpose as Kingdom citizens is to work with the King to increase the size of the first group and decrease the size of the second group. We have a responsibility to influence earthly culture with the culture of Heaven."

How well are you doing to fulfill your responsibility to influence earth's culture? Are you helping to reduce the size of the group of people who are not citizens of the Kingdom?

The Life of a Sheep, The Life of a Goat

"THE KING WILL REPLY, 'I TELL YOU THE TRUTH, WHATEVER YOU DID FOR ONE OF THE LEAST OF THESE BROTHERS OF MINE, YOU DID FOR ME'" (MATTHEW 25:40).

TODAY'S DEVOTION

Jesus told of the day when He will sit on His throne with the nations gathered for judgment. There will be two groups of people: the "sheep," or the righteous, at His right hand, and the "goats," or the unrighteous, at His left (see Matthew 25:34-46).

Jesus describes the character of the righteous, one of service and a servant heart. Humble service is so natural to those with a servant heart that they do not think of themselves as having done anything of particular merit.

Contrast this with the actions and attitude of the unrighteous, the "goats" at Jesus' left hand. The "goats" that the King addresses are not necessarily "bad" people. They may possess very high ethical and moral standards. They may be religious people. After all, they address the King as "Lord."

Kingdom culture is so different from worldly culture, that seeing it in the lives of its citizens stirs up hunger in people who are outside the Kingdom. Hunger leads to inquiry and inquiry results in new Kingdom citizens.

Service is the highest manifestation of Kingdom culture. The heart of the Kingdom of Heaven is the love of God and service is God's love in action.

(Excerpt: *Applying the Kingdom,* Chapter 10)

QUESTIONS

1. What is a "sheep" according to Jesus in Matthew 25? How does He know whether we are sheep or not?

2. What characterizes a servant heart? What is the motivation? What are the works of righteous these people display?

3. What is a "goat" according to Jesus in Matthew 25? How does He know whether we are goats, or not?

4. What characterizes a person who is not a true servant? Can these people look like servants?

5. How do true servants draw others to the Kingdom of Heaven? Are you attracting others to the Kingdom?

MEDITATION

*"Feed the hungry. Slake the thirsty. Welcome the
stranger. Clothe the naked. Tend the sick. Visit the
prisoner. These represent the heart of practical Kingdom
life. These are the same needs that most people fret
and labor for all their lives. Can you see why Christ
told us not to worry about these things? The King
provides 'all these things' to us so that we can
be His instruments in providing them to others."*

Are you actively participating in acts of service so
that you can help provide the things God has provided for you to those who do not know Him? Why
or why not?

The Motivations of Godly Service

" THEY ALSO WILL ANSWER, 'LORD, WHEN DID WE SEE YOU HUNGRY OR THIRSTY OR A STRANGER OR NEEDING CLOTHES OR SICK OR IN PRISON, AND DID NOT HELP YOU?' HE WILL REPLY, 'I TELL YOU THE TRUTH, WHATEVER YOU DID NOT DO FOR ONE OF THE LEAST OF THESE, YOU DID NOT DO FOR ME'" (MATTHEW 25:44-45).

TODAY'S DEVOTION

There are two things that make the King's nature unique. One is love. God doesn't have love, and He doesn't give love. God is love. Love is His very nature. Love means a commitment and dedication to meet another person's needs above our own.

Second, God's nature is caring. To care means "to anticipate a need and meet it; planning to meet a need before it even arises." This is the nature of the King.

Because of the loving and caring nature of God, we as Kingdom citizens must always render service out of passion and not out of a desire or expectation of pay or any other kind of public or private acknowledgment. If you love living for the King and tending to His priorities, He will see to it that you never lack a thing.

Kingdom service proceeds from the revelation of the value of every human being as a unique creation in the image of God. Kingdom service is a calling, not a career.

Service is the manifestation of the gifts God has given you. Work your gift, don't waste it. And the Bible says, your gift will make room for you in the world.

(Excerpt: *Applying the Kingdom,* Chapter 10)

QUESTIONS

1. What does it mean to you that God doesn't just have or give love, but He is love? How does His loving nature manifest itself to you?

2. How does God's caring nature manifest itself in your life? How does His care show itself over all of mankind? Why don't people recognize much of His care?

3. Why should Kingdom citizens serve out of passion and not out of some other expectation? How do we develop the passion to serve?

4. Do you love living for the King? Does the King bring true purpose to your life? Do you remember this purpose throughout your day?

5. What is the difference between a calling and a career? Is your gift being used to serve the Kingdom of God? How does God make room for that gift?

MEDITATION

"Our service also must be motivated by love and not the limelight. Most of the work of service, including the most difficult work, takes place in secret, far from the public eye and the news media. The King sees what you do in secret and His judgment is the only one that matters. Serve the King with a whole and undivided heart. Work because you love God and because you love people."

Are you regularly doing secret acts of kindness? Do you anonymously give to others? Ask God to reveal where there are opportunities for you to make His Kingdom shine.

The Process of
Entering the Kingdom

"THE LAW AND THE PROPHETS WERE PRO-
CLAIMED UNTIL JOHN. SINCE THAT TIME,
THE GOOD NEWS OF THE KINGDOM OF GOD IS BEING
PREACHED, AND EVERYONE IS FORCING HIS WAY INTO
IT" (LUKE 16:16).

TODAY'S DEVOTION

Jesus said in Matthew 6:33, that we should seek first the Kingdom and righteousness of God. Jesus said there are some great benefits that will be added free to all who set their minds to seek the Kingdom above all other priorities.

Jesus never said, "Seek Me first." He said, "Seek first the Kingdom." If you want to attract people to your country, you have to show them how and why your country is better than theirs; prove to them that they can get benefits in your country that they cannot get in their own. The Church keeps talking only about Jesus and not about the Kingdom and wonders why so few people are interested.

Jesus Christ is not the Kingdom; He is the King. Anyone who wishes to enter the Kingdom of Heaven must go in through the Door, which is Jesus. But you don't draw people to your country by talking about the port of entry. You draw them by selling them on what lies beyond the port of entry—the country's benefits and quality of life—by stirring up such a hunger and desire for the country that they will do anything to get in.

(Excerpt: *Applying the Kingdom,* Chapter 11)

QUESTIONS

1. Why do you think Jesus asked us to seek the Kingdom and not Himself? What does seeking the Kingdom entail?

2. What are some phrases and words that you can use to describe the wonderful benefits of the Kingdom? Is there someone you can practice on this week?

3. What are some specific ways that the Kingdom of God is better than any earthly nation? What are some specific ways where you have experienced the Kingdom life that would benefit some of the people around you?

4. Why do you think the Church has spoken about Jesus and virtually ignored the Kingdom? What do you think needs to happen so that we can learn to change our methods of outreach?

5. What does it mean that Jesus is the doorway to the Kingdom? If we are promoting the Kingdom in our evangelistic efforts, what do we need to share about Jesus?

MEDITATION

"People really are not looking for Jesus. They are looking for a good life. Open their eyes to the reality of the Kingdom and their focus will change. Who wouldn't trade the rat race pursuit of things for a Kingdom that guarantees all those things free and without frustration? Once a person understands what the Kingdom is, and the riches, benefits, and joys it affords, he or she will do anything to get in."

Does this information change the way you look at your evangelism techniques? What benefits of the Kingdom have you experienced personally that will make people want what you have?

The Priority of God for Mankind

"AND I CONFER ON YOU A KINGDOM, JUST AS MY FATHER CONFERRED ONE ON ME..." (LUKE 22:29).

TODAY'S DEVOTION

The Kingdom of Heaven is the most important thing on earth. It is the treasure, the pearl, the yeast, the light, and the salt of the earth.

The kingdom of heaven is like treasure hidden in a field. When a man found it, he hid it again, and then in his joy went and sold all he had and bought that field. Again, the kingdom of heaven is like a merchant looking for fine pearls. When he found one of great value, he went away and sold everything he had and bought it (Matthew 13:44-46).

Jesus said that the Kingdom of Heaven is like treasure that is so precious and so valuable that it is worth giving up everything else just to possess it. It is amazing how much people are willing to risk on even the smallest chance of striking pay dirt.

We are supposed to pursue the Kingdom even to and through the point of personal danger because once we enter it we've got it made. If we are willing to take such chances for earthly treasure that will pass away, how much more willing should we be to risk everything for the sake of gaining the Kingdom.

(Excerpt: *Applying the Kingdom,* Chapter 11)

QUESTIONS

1. Think through some of the pictures Jesus gave of the Kingdom. How is the kingdom like a pearl? How is it like yeast? How is the Kingdom a light? How is the Kingdom salt to the earth?

2. How willing are most Kingdom citizens ready to sell all for the Kingdom of God? How valuable do you think most people see the Kingdom to be? How valuable is it to you?

3. Have you ever risked your life, or perhaps your career, or perhaps your reputation for the Kingdom of God? Have you risked these for something else? What is necessary for us to make such a risk?

4. As you look over the relationships in your life, which people are firmly embedded as citizens in the Kingdom? Which people are "not far" from the Kingdom and need to see your Kingdom benefits?

5. Is there something that the Church needs to do to become exemplary of the Kingdom of God for the world to see? How will this attract people to the Kingdom?

MEDITATION

"The Kingdom of Heaven is like a precious pearl that a merchant found and then sold everything he had to buy it. That's how precious the Kingdom is. It is worth any price. Apparently the merchant had nothing left after buying the pearl except the pearl, and that was enough. So it is with the Kingdom. When we have the Kingdom, that is enough. Everything is in the Kingdom. We don't need anything else."

Have you ever lost something very valuable and searched for it vigorously? Do you see the Kingdom's value in light of how diligently you would seek for it?

The Priority of Jesus

THIS, THEN, IS HOW YOU SHOULD PRAY: "OUR FATHER IN HEAVEN, HALLOWED BE YOUR NAME, YOUR KINGDOM COME, YOUR WILL BE DONE ON EARTH AS IT IS IN HEAVEN" (MATTHEW 6:9–10).

TODAY'S DEVOTION

Jesus' only priority on earth was the Kingdom of Heaven. He taught us that the Kingdom should be our highest priority also, even in our prayers.

Notice that Jesus says that this is how we should pray. We should pray for God's Kingdom to come on earth. We should pray for His will to be done. He never says that we should pray for Him to come. Yet that is just what the Church has prayed for centuries. Jesus will return one day, and it will be a blessed day when He does, but that is not how He told us to pray. The focus of our prayers should be that the Kingdom of Heaven should come, that the influence of Heaven's government should permeate the nations and cultures of the earth like yeast in dough.

In Luke's account of Jesus' last supper with His disciples the night before He was crucified, Jesus says at one point, "I confer on you a kingdom, just as my Father conferred one on Me" (Luke 22:29). That is a political statement. Every government, when appointing ambassadors, uses the word "confer." The Kingdom is Jesus' top priority, and it must be ours as well.

(Excerpt: *Applying the Kingdom*, Chapter 11)

QUESTIONS

1. What do you think it means to pray "Thy kingdom come"? How does the Kingdom come to earth? What from Heaven comes here?

2. What do you think it means to pray "Thy will be done on earth as it is in heaven"? What is God's will in Heaven? How can it come to earth?

3. Look at the author's statement: "The focus of our prayers should be that the Kingdom of Heaven should come, that the influence of Heaven's government should permeate the nations and cultures of the earth like yeast in dough." Do you see the church making this the focus of prayer? Is this the focus of your prayer life?

4. As you look over the relationships with the people in your life, which people are firmly embedded as citizens in the Kingdom? Which are "not far" from the Kingdom and need to see your Kingdom benefits?

5. What does the fact that Jesus conferred on you the Kingdom mean? What is the nature of the conference? What responsibilities does this have on your life?

MEDITATION

"Religion postpones the Kingdom to a future experience, which is why you don't hear much about the Kingdom in religion. You cannot appropriate what you postpone. If you say the Kingdom is coming later, you can never experience it now. However, God's desire is for you to enter and experience the Kingdom right now."

Had you ever thought the Kingdom of God was a future experience and not for your life today? Discovering the Kingdom is for today should affect the way we live. In what ways should we change?

Entering the Kingdom

JESUS ANSWERED, "I TELL YOU THE TRUTH, NO ONE CAN ENTER THE KINGDOM OF GOD UNLESS HE IS BORN OF WATER AND THE SPIRIT. FLESH GIVES BIRTH TO FLESH, BUT THE SPIRIT GIVES BIRTH TO SPIRIT. YOU SHOULD NOT BE SURPRISED AT MY SAYING, 'YOU MUST BE BORN AGAIN.' THE WIND BLOWS WHEREVER IT PLEASES. YOU HEAR ITS SOUND, BUT YOU CANNOT TELL WHERE IT COMES FROM OR WHERE IT IS GOING. SO IT IS WITH EVERYONE BORN OF THE SPIRIT" (JOHN 3:5-8).

TODAY'S DEVOTION

For better understanding of entering the Kingdom, let's consider three statements that Jesus made. First, "I tell you the truth, unless you change and become like little children, you will never enter the kingdom of heaven" (Matt. 18:3). Jesus was saying that when we come into the Kingdom, we should simply live like we're in it.

Next Jesus spoke to a rich young man who asked Him what to do to receive eternal life: "There is only one who is good. If you want to enter life, obey the commandments" (Matt. 19:17b). You must obey Kingdom laws. Otherwise you may find yourself cut off from Kingdom resources and bowing under Kingdom judgment.

Jesus made the third statement right after the rich young man went away sad because he was unable to part with his wealth in order to follow Jesus: "I tell you the truth, it is hard for a rich man to enter the kingdom of heaven" (Matt. 19:23b). If you come into the Kingdom through the new birth in Christ but do not surrender your mindset of ownership, you will be unable to experience the fullness of Kingdom life because you are trying to hoard instead of releasing.

(Excerpt: *Applying the Kingdom*, Chapter 11)

QUESTIONS

1. Think through the first of Jesus' statements in Matthew 18:3. What is part of the Kingdom? What isn't? What is the goal?

2. Think through the second of Jesus' statements in Matthew 19:7b. What is part of the Kingdom? What isn't? What is the goal?

3. Think through the third of Jesus' statements in Matthew 19:23b. What is part of the Kingdom? What isn't? What is the goal?

4. Looking over the three statements and your notes in the three questions above, what misconceptions have you had about the Kingdom of God? What revelation do you receive as to what the Kingdom really is?

5. Looking over the three statements and your notes in the first three questions, what do you need to pursue in order to align your life with Kingdom principles? How will this make your life attractive to those who are outside the Kingdom?

MEDITATION

"Religion can prevent Kingdom life because religion pretends to be a substitute. Anyone who thinks the substitute is the real thing will miss out on the real thing. Unfortunately, there are many people trapped in 'religious' Christianity who believe that what they have is all there is, yet they know next to nothing about the Kingdom. They cannot enter into something they know nothing about."

Had you ever thought the Kingdom of God was a future experience and not for your life today? Discovering the Kingdom is for today should affect the way we live. In what ways should we change?

Additional copies of this book and other
book titles from DESTINY IMAGE are
available at your local bookstore.

For a complete list of our titles,
visit us at www.destinyimage.com
Send a request for a catalog to:

Destiny Image® Publishers, Inc.
P.O. Box 310
Shippensburg, PA 17257-0310

*"Speaking to the Purposes of God for This
Generation and for the Generations to Come."*

**For a complete list of our titles,
visit us at www.destinyimage.com.**

Made in United States
Orlando, FL
17 May 2024